T0209974

Water is Faithful

Haiku for Mind, Body, and Soul

CYNTHIA WILKENING

WESTBOW
PRESS®
A DIVISION OF THOMAS NELSON
& ZONDERVAN

WestBow Press books may be ordered through booksellers or by contacting:

WestBow Press
A Division of Thomas Nelson & Zondervan
1663 Liberty Drive
Bloomington, IN 47403
www.westbowpress.com
844-714-3454

ISBN: 978-1-6642-8569-9 (sc)
ISBN: 978-1-6642-8568-2 (e)

Library of Congress Control Number: 2022922192

Print information available on the last page.

WestBow Press rev. date: 1/10/2023

Water is Faithful is dedicated to my dear husband, Doug,
who brought us to a church
to meet people,
and
we met Jesus in a whole new way.

He said to me: "It is done. I am the Alpha and the Omega, the Beginning and the End. To the thirsty I will give water without cost from the spring of the water of life."
Revelation 21:6 (NIV)

Acknowledgments

I especially thank Maurice J. Reynolds, owner-editor of the online Christian poetry magazine, *Creative Inspirations,* for publishing three of my poems in his May–June 2022 issue (which are included in this book with permission: "Something from Nothing," "Too Busy, You Say," and, "There's Little Silence") and three poems in his July–August 2022 issue (which are included in this book with permission: "You'll Find If You Are," "On Another Earth," and, "Oft He Allows Storms").

Thanks go to my husband, Doug, for his support and guidance and thorough proofreading of the manuscript.

Thank you to the staff at WestBow Press for their enthusiasm for this poetry project and attention to details.

Introduction

Haiku is a form of Japanese poetry with a three-line, five-seven-five-syllable structure that traditionally focuses on nature. *Water is Faithful* retains this structure but has an overarching theme of God as a loving unit: Father, Son, and Holy Spirit. God wants family, and many of these poems express this incredible cosmic desire. The poems explore the time before time, the beginning, observations of human nature and the natural world, evil, and the God-Man, Jesus Christ of Nazareth. He meets us where we are and pursues us with a love that will not quit.

I pray that when you read this book, you will find that hope is not lost and that a relationship with the divine is not only possible but compelling.

December 2022

Something from nothing
only God could do it right
Spirit births matter

God's zeal can do it
He lives far out of the box
do not hem Him in

In the beginning
light shone before the sunshine
Spirit broke darkness

Space and time move us
spirit realm has a presence
Jesus makes it known

On another earth
they ate from the tree of life
paradise always

Adam and Eve's breath
blown in by whisper of God
passed on to babies

Man is not so smart
our perceptions limit us
blind us with knowledge

**Grace is knowing that
we cannot save ourselves from
our human nature**

**Serendipity
placed in minds that are ready
signature of God**

The angelic host
bursts with joy, birth of a boy
breaking through to earth

God a babe disguised
crying out at birth, life, death
come to Me, people!

Have you not been charmed
by the love of our God-Man?
Dying to kill death!

Spending time costs much
but time they will remember
more than all your gifts

**Some tea and crackers
in a joyful home outlasts
all technology**

Love is an action
whirring like a fan gently
so the flame is bright

Fast pace, the rat race
but character takes some time
not all comes quickly

Skin is waterproof
shedding beads of dew and rain
a common wonder

**Are you not fearful
of life beyond without love?
God beckons us now**

What does it take now
to penetrate the veiled mind
closed to God-dreaming?

I want it right now
but time cannot be rushed through
it's not always quick

Computers had bugs
but once had no viruses
a man's joke birthed sin

It started as thought
that grew to evil action
guard your inner mind

There is no evil?
Lampshades were made of man's skin
skulls in killing fields

We're caught in the web
black widow killing its mate
evil haunts money

Hatred is evil
only God's love fights its strength
breaking hate's power

**Wrath is not hatred
it is the righteous anger
of a jealous God**

I'm glad God is love
one day hate will not exist
swallowed by Spirit

Too busy, you say
"This God stuff is foolishness"
then one day you break

Jesus came to earth
to nail His life to the cross
sin debt paid in full

First impression—blink!
you're a snapshot in my mind
my collection grows

Laugh at yourself more
your smiles will spread to others
making their day glow

Don't fret about those
who crossed you during the day
they've forgotten you

The emerging plant
green leaves packed inside the seed
common miracle

A robin listens
moves its head from side to side
then delves for a worm

The stress of small winds
keeps the tree green and supple
lest the big winds blow

Summer scents, remnants
of childhood picnics with love
of family and friends

**Winter sunshine light
hangs low in the sky at three
cozy night hearkens**

Hope theme in new year
petals float, marching bands play
love springs eternal

Childlike not childish
wide-eyed with awe and delight
we recapture love

The stars are hidden
man-made light obscures God light
constellations gone

We're losing God's world
what will it be like if all
lions are captive?

God's world is dying
cities spring where springs
once flowed
He may want it back

Work should be holy
entrusting our time to God
not a trial to pass

Once crises of faith
now landmarks of the journey
Spirit rises forth

Bitter winter cold
wraps around the homeless ones
they seek a warm grate

Jesus's hands, feet
pierced for our body and soul
wounds still linger on

Weights stress the muscles
breaking down and building up
greater weights next time

Tired eyes and thoughts
when will rest meet my spirit?
Jesus pours out love

He knows what we ask
before we pray anything
spirit joins Spirit

Praying together
joins us mind to mind in trust
promises upheld

Jesus loves nature
humankind and tree rivers
someday restored whole

Wooded trails, highways,
hallways are all corridors
paths to where we stand

Delightful, winged flight
the bird swoops from feeder peak
to seed tray with grace

Sweet foods have a grip
deeply taunting my taste buds
soon to pass to self

The peoples eat bread
a basic of most cultures
fashioned many ways

Cauliflower brain
hemispheres of white matter
consciousness explained

Hang onto the Rock
He killed the enemy death
a friend worth having

If I don't write down
what I am thinking right now
thoughts gone forever

Shopping a release
but a Sabbath rest helps us
enjoy what we have

**You cannot borrow
from tomorrow's hours, they pass
for today only**

Dad's spirit left him
same chemicals as before
but life is now gone

Analyze, dissect
living things to understand
essence is then lost

Jesus won the fight
in the Garden of Olives
drops of blood, Satan

Jesus calms the storm
His power knows no limits
rest in Him safely

You'll find if you are
honest with the little things
there's trust with big things

Black is white is black
you ought not make assumptions
we are all unique

**Pigeonhole people
we can't know you otherwise
might discover souls!**

Black holes don't scare me
the spark of Jesus's touch
makes light shine again

Oft He allows storms
He tests the waters of souls
learn from Him always

Soft petal blossoms
floating in inky darkness
waters near my spirit

Afterword

Much of this book was written while commuting by train to work in Boston. I kept a small notebook handy for times when an idea popped into my head. Sometimes it was just a word that came to mind, and I'd work on it later. But sometimes, the whole poem was written down.

I am indebted to Linda and Bill for their patient and thorough introduction early on to Christian teachings and beliefs and the importance of reading the Bible. I often spent mornings on the train reading God's Word. I am not sure how many times I have read the scriptures from cover to cover, but it has been many In addition to this informal reading, I participated in and, as I grew, led Bible studies.

I am indebted to Pastor Russ, who taught many outstanding lessons and baptized me in 1992. Pastor Russ's late wife, Donna, prayed and taught me to pray through difficult situations in life. I am also indebted to Pastor Dave and his wife, René, for years of teaching through sermons, prayers, Bible studies, and just being there through some tough times.

I also thank Linda, the director of by design ministries, a New England–based organization for women church leaders. I took many sponsored classes, some taught by professors at Gordon-Conwell Seminary. I also enjoy companionship and spiritual support through monthly ladies' Together Groups. One of the ladies, Valerie Borgal, recently published a book with WestBow Press (*The Wonder of It All:*

Revealed through Poetry and Art). She directed me to WestBow and gave me a lot of pointers!

I would especially like to thank a then fourteen-year-old autistic young man who blurted out in Sunday school class, "Jesus is the singularity!"

I paused and then answered, "You might just be on to something!" I didn't hear anything more about this from him, but his insight inspired the poem about singularity at the beginning of the book.

Studying the Bible alone and in a group, and learning from sermons and conversations with other Christians, have all grounded me and taught me how best to live. I had previously been biblically illiterate and had let my mind, body, and soul run wild. I thank Jesus that I answered His knock on the door of my heart, making Him my Savior and my ultimate and loving boss.

Finally, I thank Jesus for his cosmic matchmaking in bringing Doug Wilkening into my life. Doug has supported my poetry writing from the beginning, and he gives me moral support when times get rough. He is also a witty, loving, and steadfast partner. Together, we make a good team to bring you the love of Jesus through haiku for mind, body, and soul.

Printed in the United States
by Baker & Taylor Publisher Services